1

College Vocabulary

HOUGHTON MIFFLIN
ENGLISH FOR ACADEMIC SUCCESS

Julie Howard

SERIES EDITORS

Patricia Byrd
Joy M. Reid
Cynthia M. Schuemann

Houghton Mifflin Company
Boston   New York

Publisher: Patricia A. Coryell
Director of ESL Publishing: Susan Maguire
Senior Development Editor: Kathy Sands Boehmer
Editorial Assistant: Evangeline Bermas
Senior Project Editor: Kathryn Dinovo
Manufacturing Assistant: Karmen Chong
Senior Marketing Manager: Annamarie Rice
Marketing Assistant: Andrew Whitacre

Cover graphics: LMA Communications, Natick, Massachusetts

Photo credits: © Royalty-Free/Corbis, p.1; © Patrik Giardino/Corbis, p. 16;
© Chuck Savage/Corbis, p. 32; © Ariel Skelley/Corbis, p. 48;
© James A. D'Addio/Corbis, p. 62; © Tom Stewart/Corbis, p. 76.

Printed in the U.S.A.

Library of Congress Control Number: 2004112194

ISBN: 0-618-23024-6

123456789-EUH-08 07 06 05 04

Contents

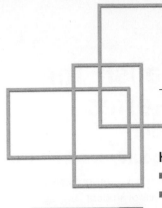

Houghton Mifflin English for Academic Success Series
- What is the Vocabulary strand all about?   vii
- What student competencies are covered in *College Vocabulary 1–4*?

Houghton Mifflin English for Academic Success Series

What Is the Vocabulary Strand All About?

The Houghton Mifflin English for Academic Success series is a comprehensive program of student and instructor materials. There are four levels of student language proficiency textbooks in three skill areas (oral communication, reading, and writing) and a supplemental vocabulary textbook at each level. Knowing how to learn and use academic vocabulary is a fundamental skill for college students. Even students with fluency in conversational English need to become effective at learning academic words for their college courses. All of the textbooks in the Houghton Mifflin English for Academic Success (EAS) series include work on vocabulary as part of academic reading, academic writing, and academic oral communication. In addition, this series provides four Vocabulary textbooks that focus on expanding student academic vocabulary and their skills as vocabulary learners. These textbooks can be used alone or can be combined with a reading, writing, or oral communication textbook. When used with one of the textbooks in the Houghton Mifflin English for Academic Success series, the vocabulary textbooks can be provided at a reduced cost and shrink-wrapped with the reading, writing, or oral communication books.

Academic vocabulary involves two kinds of words: (1) general academic vocabulary that is used in many different disciplines, and (2) highly technical words that are limited to a particular field of study. As they prepare for academic study, students need first to learn generally used academic words. A list of the general academic words called the Academic Word List (AWL) has been published by Averil Coxhead.[1] Coxhead organizes AWL words into lists based on word families, defining a *word family* as a set of related words.

The Vocabulary textbooks prepare students for their academic study by teaching them the meanings and uses of the AWL words. The AWL word families are divided among the four textbooks with each book presenting approximately 143 word families. To see the word lists for each book, visit the website for the vocabulary series at www.college.hmco.com/esl/students.

Learning new words is more effective when words are studied in meaningful contexts. Each chapter in the Vocabulary series contextualizes a set of approximately 25–30 AWL words in a "carrier topic" of interest to students. The carrier topics are intended to make the study more interesting as well as to provide realistic contexts for the words being studied. Learning a new word means learning its meaning, pronunciation, spelling, uses, and related members of the word's family. To help students with these learning challenges, the Vocabulary textbooks provide multiple encounters with words in a wide variety of activity types.

1. The AWL was introduced to the TESL/TEFL world with Coxhead's *TESOL Quarterly* publication: Coxhead, A. (2000). A new academic word list. *TESOL Quarterly 34*(2); 213–238. Coxhead is also the author of the *Essentials of Teaching Academic Vocabulary*, a teacher-reference book in the Houghton Mifflin English for Academic Success series.

Each chapter has been structured to incorporate learning strategies or tips that will help students become active acquirers and collectors of words. Additionally, because research supports the idea that multiple exposures are of great significance in learning vocabulary, each word family is practiced repeatedly and many are recycled in the lessons and chapters that follow their introduction. Newly introduced vocabulary appears in **bold** type. Recycled vocabulary is indicated by a dotted underline .

Student websites for the Vocabulary textbooks provide additional practice with the AWL words as well as useful review chapters. Instructors and students can download these review chapters for use as homework or in-class study. The website for each book expands the practice with the AWL words covered in that book. Students can access vocabulary flash cards for the complete 570 word families if they choose to work with words beyond those introduced in the particular vocabulary textbook they are studying. Each of these flash cards has the AWL word, its definition, and an example.

Although, with the addition of online answer keys, this book can be an aid to self-study, it is ideally suited for classroom use. According to the focus of your course, you may choose to have your students respond to some of the exercises in writing, while you may choose to make oral activities of others. Of course, you can also incorporate practice in both skills by following oral discussion with a writing assignment. You may ask students to work individually on some exercises, while others will be better suited to pair or small-group configurations.

Acknowledgments

With sincere gratitude to Houghton Mifflin staff Susan Maguire and Kathy Sands Boehmer for their patience and enthusiastic support; to series editors Pat Byrd, Joy Reid, and Cynthia Schuemann for their faith and wisdom; and to my fellow vocabulary series authors for their generosity and collaboration.

I'd also like to thank my reviewers: Patricia Appel, American River College; Shannon Bailey, Austin Community College; Sean Dugan, Mercy College; Kathleen Huggard, LaGuardia Community College; and Lorraine Segal, Napa Valley College; and adjunct advisors Eric Bohman and Cynthia Comstock.

▭ What Student Competencies Are Covered in *College Vocabulary 1–4*?

Description of Overall Purposes

Students develop the ability to understand and use words from the Academic Word List (AWL) that are frequently encountered in college course work.

Materials in this textbook are designed with the following minimum exit objectives in mind:

Competency 1: The student will recognize the meaning of selected academic vocabulary words.

Competency 2: The student will demonstrate controlled knowledge of the meaning of selected academic vocabulary words.

Competency 3: The student will demonstrate active use of selected academic vocabulary words.

Competency 4: The student will develop and apply strategies for vocabulary learning. The student will:
a. recognize roots, affixes, and inflected forms.
b. distinguish among members of word families.
c. identify and interpret word functions.
d. recognize and manipulate appropriate collocations.
e. use contextual clues to aid understanding.
f. develop word learning resources such as flash cards and personal lists.
g. increase awareness of how words are recycled in written text and oral communication.
h. increase awareness of the benefits of rehearsal for word learning (repetition and reuse of words in multiple contexts).

Competency 5: The student will use dictionaries for vocabulary development and to distinguish among multiple meanings of a word.

Competency 6: The student will analyze words for syllable and stress patterns and use such analysis to aid in correct pronunciation.

Competency 7: The student will analyze words for spelling patterns.

Competency 8: The student will become familiar with web-based resources for learning AWL words.

1

Dictionaries and Word Study

ex·cep'tion·à·ble
exceptionable.
ex·cep'tion·à·bly,
manner.
ex·cep'tion·ăl, *a.* r
ception; out of th
uncommon; ext
talent.

In this chapter, you will

- Become familiar with twenty-two academic vocabulary words
- Practice using a dictionary to study different aspects of vocabulary, such as parts of speech and word families
- Practice putting words in alphabetical order
- Notice when words that were introduced earlier are repeated
- Notice whether nouns are count or noncount
- Begin making and using flash cards to test your memory of vocabulary words
- Read about the most common of all reference books, the dictionary, and how it is helpful in learning words

Section 1

EXERCISE 1 Use a dictionary as needed to help you fill in Word List 1.1. Practice the pronunciations of the words with your instructor or a partner. Write the meanings in the chart now or after you finish Exercise 2. Two items have been filled in for you as examples.

WORD LIST 1.1

Word	POS	Meaning	Example
series			A **series** of earthquakes shook the city.
chapter		*a part of something, such as a book*	The instructor assigned a **chapter** of the book for homework.
authority			She is an **authority** on antique jewelry.
definition			The **definition** of *rapid* is "fast."
relevant			You must be at least sixteen to drive in Illinois. Age is **relevant**.
investment	n.		Learning a language is an **investment** of time and effort.
communication			**Communication** in a second language is often difficult.

EXERCISE 2   Read the passage. For each word in **bold**, circle the choice in parentheses ( ) that is nearer in meaning. Use a dictionary as needed.

USING DICTIONARIES TO LEARN ABOUT WORDS

Today you are beginning the first in a **series** (a television program that airs each week / a number of things that follow one after another) of four vocabulary books that will help you learn the words that most often appear in college course readings. This **chapter** (page of a book / part of a book) discusses one of the most useful tools a student of words can have—a dictionary. A dictionary is a generally accepted **authority** (a thing or person with expert information / a book that is correct) on the use of words.

When you use dictionaries, it is often to find the **definitions** (meanings / specifications) of words. However, dictionaries provide much more information than that. For example, they almost always tell you how to pronounce a word by using a system of symbols for different sounds, by indicating how many syllables a word has, and by showing which syllable is stressed. Dictionaries usually include other **relevant** (related / dependent) information, such as other members of a word's family, drawings or photographs, and sample sentences in which the words are used.

A dictionary created especially for English language learners will probably be most helpful to you. A good dictionary, or even two or three, is an excellent **investment** (something spent for future benefit / a stock that is publicly traded) that will pay you back many times by helping you improve your **communication** (exchange of ideas and information / conversation by telephone or in person) skills.

Master Student Tip

Beginning with the seven words in Word List 1.1 and continuing throughout this book, make a flash card for each word. Write each vocabulary word on one side of a three-by-five-inch card. Write the meaning of the word on the other side. Use the cards to test yourself or a partner. You may add other information to each card—for example, a corresponding word in your first language, a sample sentence, or the pronunciation of the word.

EXERCISE **3**   Make flash cards for the seven vocabulary words in Word List 1.1.

EXERCISE **4**   Write T if the sentence is true, or F if it is false. Change the sentences that are false to make them true. The first one has been done for you as an example.

1. ___T___ Putting money in the stock market is an **investment**.

2. _____ Your instructor is an **authority** on the English language for you.

3. _____ A **definition** is the pronunciation of the word.

4. _____ **Communication** can happen on the Internet.

5. _____ How a word is spelled is not **relevant** information for a student to know.

6. _____ This exercise is a **series** of sentences that you read and think about.

7. _____ This book has eight **chapters**.

EXERCISE 5 Complete the sentences logically and grammatically with your own ideas. The first one has been done for you as an example.

1. I started a new **chapter** of my life when *I began to study at this school.*

2. My English **communication** skills _____ .

3. My favorite television comedy/drama **series** is _____

_____ .

4. _____ is an **authority** on the subject of

_____ .

5. If I had more money, I would make an **investment** in _____

_____ .

6. When buying a house/car/computer, these considerations are **relevant**:

_____ .

7. I do not speak _____ (name of language), but I know the **definition** of the word _____ . It means

_____ .

Master Student Tip

Word families are groups of related words. For example, *ease*, *easy*, *easily*, and *easier* are all members of the same word family. You can increase your vocabulary by learning the different forms in word families. A dictionary helps you recognize and learn members of word families.

EXERCISE **6** Use a dictionary as needed to fill in the verb members of the word families in the chart below. One answer has been given as an example. Remember that nouns are people, places, things, or ideas and that verbs are actions or states.

Noun	Verb
1. communication	1. *communicate*
2. definition	2.
3. investment	3.
4. authority	4.

Now, write an original sentence containing each verb in the chart above. Ask a classmate to read your sentences and offer suggestions to improve them.

1. _____

2. _____

3. _____

4. _____

Master Student Tip

Beginning with Section 2 and continuing throughout this book, vocabulary words that were introduced in earlier sections are indicated with a dotted underline. By reading these underlined words and thinking about them, you can more easily remember and use them in the future.

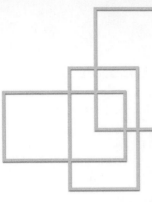

Section 2

EXERCISE 7 Use a dictionary as needed to help you fill in Word List 1.2. Practice the pronunciations of the words with your instructor or a partner. Write the meanings in the chart now or after you finish Exercise 8. Two items have been filled in for you as examples.

WORD LIST 1.2

Word	POS	Meaning	Example
versions			Computer software comes in different **versions**.
parallel			Courses at different U.S. colleges are sometimes, but not always, **parallel**.
technical			I enjoy looking at art, but I don't know much about the **technical** side of it.
concepts			Students learn new **concepts** in their classes.
previous	*adj.*		**Previous** experience in an occupation helps you get a job.
security			Good parents try to give their children a feeling of **security**.
assess		*evaluate*	It is difficult to **assess** how much of what we say a baby understands.
elements			Decorative **elements** in a home may include plants, paintings, and curtains.
approach			Memorization is one **approach** to learning vocabulary.

EXERCISE 8 Read the passage. For each word in **bold**, circle the choice in parentheses ( ) that is nearer in meaning.

TYPES AND USES OF DICTIONARIES

Most people use dictionaries to help them find the kind of general information you are studying in this chapter. Many publishers have this type of dictionary in both printed and online **versions** (forms / poetry). Generally, the hard copy and computer editions are **parallel** (matching / different) except for the forms, and they are intended for use by native or near-native speakers of the language.

Other types of dictionaries, however, are used for **technical** (difficult / specialized) needs. For example, there are dictionaries that contain information useful to businesspeople or healthcare workers. Those dictionaries define words and **concepts** (ideas / sentences) important to those professions.

Bilingual dictionaries, such as Swedish-English or Japanese-English, are especially helpful to learners in the beginning of their language studies. Perhaps you used one in your **previous** (later / earlier) study of English. Bilingual dictionaries are good because they can provide basic information quickly and can give students a feeling of **security** (safety / danger).

English-English dictionaries for learners are also important. How can you **assess** (analyze / describe) an English-English dictionary's usefulness to you? Look for **elements** (weather / parts) such as pictures, sample sentences, and special notes on usage. Look for a pronunciation guide and other useful information near the front and back of the book. Look up a few words to see if you understand the definitions. A good English dictionary for learners uses an **approach** (idea / method) that makes learning vocabulary easier.

EXERCISE 9 Make flash cards for the nine vocabulary words in Word List 1.2.

> **Master Student Tip**
>
> When studying nouns, note whether they are count or noncount. If a noun can be made plural, such as *books* and *children*, and can be counted, it is a count noun. If it cannot be counted, such as *sugar* and *information*, it is noncount. Knowing if a noun is count or noncount is necessary to using it correctly. Some nouns, such as *cake/cakes*, can be both count and noncount, depending on the situation. Noncount: *Cake* is often served at birthday parties. Count: We ordered three *cakes* for the anniversary party.

EXERCISE 10 Look at Word List 1.2 again. Then, answer these questions.

1. Of the nine vocabulary words in the list, how many are nouns? ————

2. Which noun is noncount in the example? ——————————————

3. Which three nouns are plural in the examples?

———————————————————————————————

EXERCISE 11 In each blank space, write one of the words from the word bank. Change the words for number, person, or tense if necessary. Do not use the same word twice. The first one has been done for you as an example.

security	approach	element
assess	concept	technical
version	parallel	previous

1. The twins led __*parallel*__ lives, both graduating with degrees in engineering and going to work for the same company.

2. We need to learn a lot of _____ vocabulary and many new _____ in studying about computers. We also need to learn about _____ systems so that our computer activities remain private.

3. In most college courses, the instructor _____ your performance and knowledge and gives you a grade. Attendance may be another _____ considered in assigning grades.

4. In _____ centuries, lexicographers made dictionaries by including all the words they knew and by asking the public and advisers for additional words. Today, computers make the use of a different _____ possible. Computers can analyze text and make the publication of new _____ of dictionaries much easier.

EXERCISE 12 Rearrange the letters and write the correctly spelled vocabulary words from Word List 1.2. The first one has been done for you as an example.

1. sseass   _assess_ _____

2. epcocnt   _____

3. rvoines   _____

4. urisytec   _____

5. popchara   _____

6. clatenihc   _____

7. aalllrep   _____

8. nemlete   _____

9. viseporu   _____

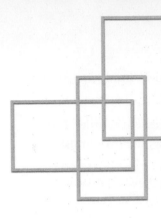

Section 3

EXERCISE 13 Use a dictionary as needed to help you fill in Word List 1.3. Practice the pronunciations of the words with your instructor or a partner. Write the meanings in the chart now or after you finish Exercise 12. Two items have been done for you as examples.

WORD LIST 1.3

Word	POS	Meaning	Example
initial		*at the beginning*	My **initial** impression of my instructor was very favorable.
components			A CD player and speakers are **components** of a stereo system.
involves			Learning vocabulary **involves** many skills.
text	n.		A **text** can be a complete book or a part of a book.
achieve			How will you **achieve** your academic goals?
target			**Targets** are used in games and sports such as darts, archery, and shooting.

EXERCISE 14 Read the sentences. For each word in **bold**, circle the choice in parentheses ( ) that is nearer in meaning.

1. Entries in English language dictionaries are in alphabetical order. If the **initial** (first / last) letters of two words are the same, then you must look at the next letters to put them in order.

2. Dictionaries help you with the many **components** (rules / parts) of word study, including spellings, definitions, word families, and pronunciations. Learning words **involves** (brings / includes) all of these elements.

3. To understand a **text** (something written / a grammar lesson), a reader must understand most of the words in it. That is why increasing vocabulary is so important. You need to know a lot of words to **achieve** (remember / succeed in) fluency, not only in reading, but also in writing and speaking.

4. The **target** (goal / weapon) of this book is vocabulary that students use in college degree program courses.

EXERCISE 15 Make flash cards for the six words in Word List 1.3.

EXERCISE 16 Work with a partner or small group to discuss these questions. Try to use the vocabulary words in your answers.

1. What would you like to **achieve** in the next ten years? What about the next twenty years? Do you have **target** dates for graduating from college, getting a good job in your profession, or other goals?

2. Compare your **initial** impressions of the United States/the city where you live/the school you attend/your job with the opinions of that place you have now. How have they changed?

3. What does being successful in school **involve**? How easy or difficult is it to do?

4. What are or were the **components** of your current/former English language program? Do/Did you attend different classes every day? What about laboratories?

5. Besides this one, what **texts** (textbooks) are you using this term? Do you like one especially? Why?

> **Master Student Tip**
>
> Dictionaries of English and of many other languages, as well as indexes in the backs of textbooks, present entries in alphabetical order: a, b, c, and so on. Being familiar with the alphabetical order of English is important in finding words quickly and easily.

EXERCISE 17 Write the six words from Word List 1.3 in alphabetical order below.

1. _____   4. _____

2. _____   5. _____

3. _____   6. _____

Now, put the following words in alphabetical order below by writing the numbers 1 through 12 in the spaces provided. One has been done for you as an example.

—— previous   —— parallel   —— perimeter   _1_ pachyderm

—— package   —— pouch   —— pretty   —— park

—— poor   —— previously   —— packet   —— pay

EXERCISE 18 Your instructor will dictate six new sentences, each of which uses a vocabulary word from Word List 1.3. He or she will repeat each sentence three times. Listen and write what you hear. After you are finished, check your sentences with your instructor.

1. _____

2. _____

3. _____

4. _____

5. _____

6. _____

Section 4

EXERCISE 19 Use the flash cards you made for the words in this chapter to test yourself or a classmate.

EXERCISE 20 Use the clues to fill in the crossword puzzle. Check the spelling of each word. This puzzle contains seventeen of the twenty-two vocabulary words in this chapter.

Across

1. Similar
7. Relating to a specialization
9. Something we put money or time in
10. Written language
12. Meaning
14. Safety
15. One thing after another
16. Goal
17. Include

Down

2. Evaluate
3. Expert
4. Idea
5. Succeed
6. Another form of the same thing
8. Earlier
11. One part among others
13. First

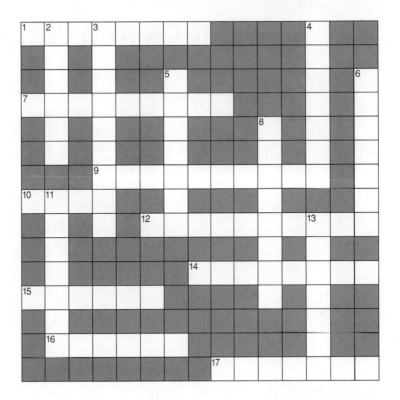

What's in a Name?

TONG

In this chapter, you will

- Become familiar with twenty-six academic vocabulary words
- Continue to make and use flash cards to test your memory of vocabulary words
- Learn about collocations, words that often occur together or near each other
- Learn how to use a dictionary to determine the number of syllables in a word and which syllable is stressed
- Read about the variety of names in the United States and customs related to names and naming

Section 1

EXERCISE 1 Use a dictionary as needed to help you fill in Word List 2.1. Practice the pronunciations of the words with your instructor or a partner. Write the meanings in the chart now or after you finish Exercise 2. Four items have been done for you as examples.

WORD LIST 2.1			
Word	**POS**	**Meaning**	**Example**
immigration			**Immigration** has made the United States a society of many cultures.
impact			Other cultures have had an **impact** on American names, foods, and clothes.
ethnic	*adj.*		**Ethnic** groups, such as African Americans, enrich American life.
prior			**Prior** experience in an occupation is an advantage in applying for a job.
sought		*past/past participle of seek, meaning "try to get" or "look for"*	Immigrants to the United States have often **sought** political and religious freedom.
shift	*v. & n.*		An earthquake is a sudden **shift** in Earth's crust.
outcomes			Scientists experiment to learn which **outcomes** are possible.
procedure			There is a **procedure** to follow in registering for college classes.
sum		*total or summary*	The **sum** of 2 + 2 is 4.
debate			Gun control is the subject of much **debate** in the United States.

EXERCISE 2 Read the passage. For each word in **bold**, circle the choice in parentheses ( ) that is nearer in meaning.

LAST NAMES IN THE UNITED STATES

Did you know that *Rodriguez* and *Gonzalez* are two of the most common family names in the United States? **Immigration** (arrival of visitors and tourists / settling of people from other countries) to the United States has had a great **impact** (effect / history) on family names in this country. In addition to Hispanics, other **ethnic** (cultural / economic) groups have made such names as *Huang/Wong* (Chinese), *Kowalski* (Polish), *Kim* (Korean), and *Martinelli* (Italian) as familiar as English names like *Smith* and *Johnson*.

Prior (after / before) to the late twentieth century, many new arrivals to the United States were encouraged to change their family names to English or Northern European ones to become "more American"; for example, *Martinelli* might be changed to *Martin*. Because they feared discrimination, many newcomers **sought** (tried / enjoyed) to blend into American society and not to attract attention by having foreign-sounding names.

Today, however, public opinion has **shifted** (disappeared / changed). Cultural heritage, countries of origin, and ancestry are matters of pride and interest, and ties to the first language and homeland are often maintained. Becoming bilingual and becoming bicultural are seen as good **outcomes** (results / things). In addition, changing one's name is a legal **procedure** (a number of problems / a way of doing something) that may involve time and money. In **sum** (summary / summer), keeping one's original family name is much easier than it used to be and is no longer the subject of much **debate** (disagreement / action).

EXERCISE 3 Make flash cards for the ten vocabulary words in Word List 2.1.

EXERCISE 4 Circle the letter (*a* or *b*) of the better, more logical completion for each item.

1. In the past, most women took their husbands' last names upon marriage. Now, attitudes have **shifted**, so
   a. many women continue to take their husbands' names.
   b. many women keep their own last names after marriage.

2. The many **ethnic** groups in the United States are the reason that
   a. there is a large variety of family names here.
   b. most of the family names here are English.

3. The fact that there is **debate** on a subject means that
   a. people usually agree on the subject.
   b. people hold different opinions about the subject.

4. Because of **immigration**,
   a. Americans know about and enjoy many kinds of foods.
   b. Americans cook and enjoy only one kind of food.

5. If we know the **outcome** of a soccer game,
   a. we know how long the game was.
   b. we know which team won the game.

6. **Prior** to his graduation from college, he
   a. worked part time at a car wash.
   b. found a job in his profession.

7. The **impact** of their visit to Italy was so great that
   a. the Porters gave their first son an Italian name.
   b. the Porters forgot their trip immediately.

> **Master Student Tip**
>
> Collocations are words often used together or located near each other. Some collocations are grammatical. For example, after the verb *enjoy*, we cannot use an infinitive (*to* + verb), but we can use a gerund (verb + *-ing*). Incorrect: I *enjoy to dance*. Correct: I *enjoy dancing*.
>
> Other collocations are semantic. Consider the verb *assassinate*, which means "murder a prominent person by surprise attack." Only a politician or other well-known leader can be *assassinated*. Incorrect: He *assassinated the mail carrier*. Correct: He *assassinated the President*. Noticing collocations helps you use words more appropriately.

EXERCISE 5 Circle the letter of the appropriate collocation—in this case, the correct preposition, that completes each sentence. You may refer to other exercises in this section as examples.

1. I had never heard the name *Mireille* **prior** _____ my visit to France.
   a. of   **b.** to

2. **Immigration** _____ the United States has resulted in a large variety of names.
   a. in   **b.** to

3. Choosing a name for a new baby may be the subject _____ **debate** between parents.
   a. of   **b.** on

4. Popular culture also has an **impact** _____ which names are given.
   a. on   **b.** of

5. In Hispanic culture, *Jesus* is a common given name for a boy. However, people of English ancestry almost never have this name. _____ **sum**, there are cultural differences with respect to this name.
   a. for   **b.** in

6. More contact with other cultures often produces a **shift** _____ public opinion of those cultures.
   a. to   **b.** in

7. Many newcomers to the United States have **sought** _____ find a better life here.
   a. to   **b.** for

EXERCISE 6 Write the best word from the word bank to complete each sentence. You may need to change forms for tense or number. Do not use the same word twice. The first one has been done for you as an example.

impact	shift	immigration	sum
prior	seek	outcome	debate
procedure			ethnic

1. There are frequent *shifts*_____ in name preferences. People born in the 1980s or later may have names like *Ashley* and *Jason*; _____ to that, Biblical names such as *Mary* and *John* were more popular.

2. Irish Americans represent a large _____ group in the United States.

3. Some people _____ to give their children original names that will be noticed and remembered.

4. The _____ of the senatorial election was announced last night.

5. The _____ followed in naming a baby may differ in different cultures. In the United States, it is usually done by the parents within a day or two after the baby is born.

6. Names like *Ahmed*, *Dmitri*, and *Midori* are familiar to many Americans because of _____.

7. In some countries, using "foreign" names is a subject of heated _____, but in the United States it is common. For example, French has had an _____ on the names Americans give their daughters. Common choices are *Michelle* and *Renee*. Muslim names, such as *Kareem* and *Abdul*, are popular among some African Americans. In _____, Americans are generally very open to using names borrowed from languages other than English.

Section 2

EXERCISE **7** Fill in Word List 2.2. Use a dictionary if needed. Practice the pronunciations of the words with your instructor or a partner. One of the words is French. Based on the pronunciation, which one do you think it is? _____ Write the meanings of the words now or after you finish Exercise 8. Three items have been done for you as examples.

WORD LIST 2.2

Word	POS	Meaning	Example
partnership			Sears and Roebuck was the original name of a retail **partnership**.
final		*last*	In English names, the **final** word is the family name. In Chinese names, it is the opposite.
phase			Joey went through a **phase** during which he wanted to be called Joseph.
consequences			It is important to think about the **consequences** of our actions.
welfare			Parents care about the **welfare** of their children.
data	*pl. n. (Sing. is datum.)*		**Data** show that the most common American surname is *Smith*.
regime	*n.*		The Soviet Union was a communist **regime**.
site			American city names, such as *Springfield*, often refer to **sites**.

EXERCISE 8 Read the sentences. For each word in **bold**, circle the choice in parentheses ( ) that is nearer in meaning.

1. Business **partnerships** (relationships in joint activities / family relationships) are often identified by family names. For example, *Brown, Castro, and Finkel* might be the name of an accounting or law firm. The **final** (first / last) name listed is typically that of the newest or least important member of the **partnership**.

2. Children or teenagers sometimes pass through a **phase** (a group of words / a stage of development) during which they do not like their given names.

3. Giving a child an unpopular name may have unplanned **consequences** (results / facts). A person's **welfare** (happiness / money from the government) and success may depend, to a certain extent, on her or his name. Research has shown that some teachers and bosses tend to expect and get better performance from those whose names they like.

4. **Data** (statistics / months and years) show that *James* and *Mary* are among the most common given names for older American men and women.

5. A male child born when his country is ruled by a dictator may be named for the leader of the **regime** (government / religion) to demonstrate his parents' loyalty or to protect the family.

6. A family name may come from a **site** (building / place). Examples are *Hill, Field, Forest, Bridge,* and *Kirk,* which is Gaelic for "church."

EXERCISE 9 Make flash cards for the eight vocabulary words in Word List 2.2.

EXERCISE 10 Write an appropriate word from the word bank to fill in each blank. You may use the same word more than once. The first one has been done for you as an example. Look at other exercises in this section if needed, to see what collocations are used.

socialist	of	scientific	between

1. the **consequences** ___of___ your actions

2. a **partnership** _____ two families

3. a _____ **regime**

4. the **site** _____ an accident

5. _____ **data**

6. the **welfare** _____ a family

EXERCISE 11 Match the parts to make logical, grammatical sentences. Write the letter of the item that best completes the first part of the sentence. One lettered item will not be used. The first one has been done for you as an example.

a. ruled through fear and violence.
b. should be the concern of a government.
c. **consequence** of her hard work.
d. are difficult to understand.
e. can be seen in the night sky.
f. item in this exercise.
g. as a **partnership** between two friends.
h. are among the **data** collected about us.
i. the 2004 Summer Olympics.

1. Ben & Jerry's ice cream company began ___g___

2. Greece was the **site** of _____

3. The authoritarian **regime** _____

4. Barbara's high salary was a natural _____

5. Our names and ages _____

6. The **welfare** of its people _____

7. The **phases** of the moon _____

8. This is the **final** _____

EXERCISE **12** Answer each question briefly, using one of the vocabulary words from Word List 2.2. Do not use the same word twice. The first one has been done for you as an example.

  1. Which word means "location"?

   site

  2. Which word could describe a good marriage?

   _____

  3. Which word is the opposite of "first"?

   _____

  4. Which word refers to the people in power in a city or country?

   _____

  5. Which word means "information"?

   _____

  6. Which word describes a temporary change in behavior?

   _____

  7. Which word describes what you want for your friends and family?

   _____

  8. Which word means "results"?

   _____

Section 3

EXERCISE 13 Fill in Word List 2.3. Use a dictionary if needed. Practice the pronunciations of the words with a partner or your instructor. Write the meanings now or after you finish Exercise 14. Two items have been done for you as examples.

WORD LIST 2.3

Word	POS	Meaning	Example
core			The temperature at Earth's **core** is very high.
occur			What **occurred** on July 4, 1776?
contract			When you buy a house, you must sign a **contract**.
civil	*adj.*		The couple was married in a **civil** ceremony at city hall.
clauses		*parts of a legal document*	Be sure to read all the **clauses** before you sign any agreement.
principles			**Principles** such as the equality of all people are important in American life.
coordination			The city government provides **coordination** of services such as water, garbage pickup, and street cleaning.
layer			In cold climates, several **layers** of lightweight clothing will keep you warmer than just one heavy layer.

EXERCISE 14 Read the sentences. For each word in **bold**, circle the choice in parentheses ( ) that is nearer in meaning. Use a dictionary as needed.

1. Our names seem to be at the **core** (center / edge) of our identity. That is why we may be bothered when mistakes **occur** (continue / happen), such as someone calling us by the wrong names or mispronouncing our names.

2. When signing a **contract** (letter / written agreement), it is important to use your legal name, the name on all your **civil** (not military or religious / expensive) documents. You may also need to write your initials next to any **clauses** (parts of a contract / parts of a sentence) that have been changed by you or by others.

3. In some cultures, **principles** (bosses or supervisors / rules or beliefs) govern the types of names that may be given to new babies. For example, given names might refer to birth order or might be the same names already given to older family members.

4. In the United States, there is no overall **coordination** (organization / communication) of naming by the government or religion. Parents are free to give any names they choose, and they may even change the traditional spellings of names to provide variety. No additional **layer** (something costing a lot of money / something lying between others) of approval stands between them and the names they prefer.

EXERCISE 15 Make flash cards for the eight vocabulary words in Word List 2.3.

Master Student Tip

The number of syllables in a word and the syllable that is stressed (the strongest syllable) are basic facts we need to know to pronounce a word correctly. Dictionaries usually separate syllables by using "bullets" (e.g., Eng•lish) or spaces (e.g., Eng lish). Sometimes the syllables related to spelling (Eng•lish), which show where you can divide a word at the end of a line of writing, differ from those related to pronunciation (e.g., ing glish). The stressed syllable is usually indicated with an accent mark (e.g., ing´glish).

EXERCISE 16 Rewrite these words. Use spaces to separate pronunciation syllables, and use accent marks (´) to show which syllables are stressed. Use a dictionary if needed. How many of the words have only one syllable? _____ Write "one syllable" after them.

1. core _____   5. clause _____

2. occur _____   6. principle _____

3. contract _____   7. coordination _____

4. civil _____   8. layer _____

EXERCISE 17 Discuss these questions with a partner or in small group.

1. Have you ever signed a **contract**? What was it for? Was it difficult to read? Did you have a lawyer look at it before you signed it? Did the **contract** contain any important **clauses**? In what kinds of situations are **contracts** used in the United States?

2. What **principles** guide your behavior and opinions? Where did your **principles** come from—your parents? your religion? your own ideas?

3. You may wear **layers** of clothing. Cakes can have **layers**. List as many other things that have **layers** as you can. Ask your instructor if your list is correct.

4. What are some important dates (day and year) in your life? What **occurred** or will **occur** on those dates? What important dates in history can you think of? What **occurred** on those dates?

5. When we eat apples, we often throw away the **cores**. What other fruits and vegetables have **cores**? Check your answers with your instructor.

6. Legal cases are sometimes divided into two categories: criminal and **civil**. Murder is criminal. What other crimes would be found in the criminal category? A divorce is a **civil** case. What other kinds of **civil** cases can you think of?

EXERCISE 18 Change the order of the words to write logical, grammatical sentences. Use each word in each group only once. The first one has been done for you as an example.

1. American / English / at / usually / colleges / is / **core** / Freshman / a / course

   Freshman English is usually a core course at American colleges.

2. important / of / in / religion / is / States / the / Freedom / an / **principle** / United

   _____

3. can / **Civil** / "polite" / mean / also

   _____

4. are / How / you / clothes / wearing / **layers** / many / today / of

   _____

5. it / before / **contract** / **clauses** / sign / Read / a / and / its / carefully / you

   _____

6. Columbus' / of / 1492 / **occurred** / America / discovery / in

   _____

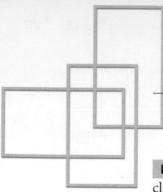

Section 4

CHAPTER 2 REVIEW

EXERCISE 19 Use the flash cards you made to test yourself or a classmate on the twenty-six words in this chapter.

EXERCISE 20 Match each bold word with its definition. Write the appropriate letter in the blank. The first one has been done for you as an example. Two of the lettered definitions will not be used.

1. __h__ **final**

2. _____ **principle**

3. _____ **shift**

4. _____ **ethnic**

5. _____ **phase**

6. _____ **outcome**

7. _____ **debate**

8. _____ **occur**

9. _____ **sought**

10. _____ **contract**

11. _____ **site**

12. _____ **prior**

13. _____ **data**

14. _____ **core**

a. discussion
b. result
c. before
d. looked for
e. move
f. center
g. happiness
h. last
i. location
j. stage
k. safety
l. happen
m. belief
n. information
o. cultural
p. agreement

EXERCISE 21 Rewrite these words. Use spaces to separate pronunciation syllables, and use accent marks (´) to show which syllables are stressed. Refer to Exercise 16 in this chapter for a model. Use a dictionary if needed.

1. procedure _____

2. consequence _____

3. impact _____

4. partnership _____

5. regime _____

6. sum _____

7. welfare _____

8. immigration _____

WEB POWER

You will find additional exercises related to the content in this chapter at **http://esl.college.hmco.com/students.**

Consumer Education

In this chapter, you will

- Become familiar with thirty academic vocabulary words
- Identify and practice using some words that function as both nouns and verbs with no changes
- Continue to make and use flash cards to test your memory of vocabulary words
- Read about some ways that businesses and manufacturers use to attract consumers (buyers and users) to their products, and become familiar with aspects of consumer education that help people make good decisions when they shop

Section 1

> **Master Student Tip**
>
> Knowing the part of speech of a word (such as whether the word is a noun or a verb) helps you understand and use the word appropriately. As you learn new words, note the part of speech for each.

EXERCISE 1 Use a dictionary to help you fill in Word List 3.1. Four words may function as both nouns and verbs. One is indicated for you. Which one is it? _____. What are the other three?

_____, _____, _____.

Practice the pronunciations of the words with your instructor or a partner. Write the meanings in the chart now or after you finish Exercise 2. Two items have been done for you as examples.

WORD LIST 3.1

Word	POS	Meaning	Example
design			Architects **design** houses and other buildings.
purchase	*n. and v.*		You can **purchase** a computer at an electronics store.
focus			To increase your vocabulary, you must **focus** on new words.
section			Socks can usually be found near the shoe **section** of a store.
option			Jogging and swimming are **options** for people who like to exercise.
select		*choose*	Some people **select** schools on the basis of recommendations from their friends.
identify			Can you **identify** the part of speech of this word?

Word	POS	Meaning	Example
location			A good **location** attracts shoppers to a store.
label			The **label** in a shirt tells its size and where it was made.
considerable			Many large cars use a **considerable** amount of gasoline.

Master Student Tip

Do not hesitate to use a dictionary to help you understand the meaning of vocabulary words. You may want to look up words in both bilingual and English-English dictionaries.

EXERCISE 2 Read the following passage. For each bold word, circle the choice in parentheses ( ) that is nearer in meaning. Use a dictionary as needed.

AT THE SUPERMARKET

The next time you enter a large American supermarket, take a careful look around you. The entire place has been **designed** (planned / painted) to make you want to **purchase** (see / buy) as much as possible, and the **focus** (purpose / shape) of every can, bottle, and box is on attracting you and your dollars.

Go to the breakfast cereal **section** (area / shelf) and notice how many **options** (choices / brands) are there. Usually there are dozens, making it difficult to **select** (take / choose) just one. Now look at the packages. Which ones can be **identified** (known / included) as children's cereals? They are often colorful and decorated with cartoon characters. Notice their **location** (place / size) in relation to other cereals. Typically, they are placed on shelves at a child's eye level from the ground or from the child's seat of a shopping cart. Read the nutritional **labels** (lists of contents / numbers) on the boxes of children's cereals. Usually, these cereals contain sugar, which is popular with children.

After visiting just this one part of the supermarket, you can see that **considerable** (much / little) thought, planning, and effort have been put into getting the attention and influencing the decisions of shoppers.

EXERCISE 3 Make flash cards for the ten vocabulary words in Word List 3.1.

Master Student Tip

Many English words can function as both nouns and verbs. Knowing which words can be both nouns and verbs will increase your vocabulary.

EXERCISE 4 Read each sentence. In each case, decide whether the bold word is used as a *noun* (a person, place, thing, or idea) or a *verb* (an action or state of being). Write *n.* (noun) or *v.* (verb) above each bold word to tell how it is used in the sentence. Be prepared to explain to your classmates how you made each decision.

1. Shoppers generally make more **purchases** before and during holidays.

2. Few people are able to **purchase** a house with cash.

3. The **label** on a product gives important information about it.

4. Food products must be **labeled** with their ingredients.

5. Companies **design** packages to attract the attention of shoppers.

6. Sales improved when the company used a more colorful **design** for its package.

7. Consumers should **focus** on value and quality when making decisions.

8. Toys are often the **focus** of Saturday morning television commercials.

EXERCISE 5 Match the parts to make logical, grammatical sentences. Write the letter of the item that best completes the first part of the sentence. One lettered item will not be used. The first one has been done for you as an example.

a. **focus** on what you need.
b. is a **considerable** expense.
c. is too expensive for most people.
d. products made for children.
e. because of its **location**.
f. because of its packaging.

g. look at the date on the bag.
h. tells what is in it.
i. many **options**.
j. decisions shoppers make.
k. has pens and notebooks.

1. The **label** on a can of soup ___h___

2. To **select** a fresh loaf of bread _____

3. Buying food for a large family _____

4. Some consumers **purchase** food _____

5. The school supplies **section** _____

6. We sometimes choose a store _____

7. Large supermarkets generally have _____

8. Making a list will help you _____

9. Store **design** may influence _____

10. It is not difficult to **identify** _____

EXERCISE 6   Use your own words and ideas to complete each sentence logically and grammatically.

1. When I shop, I try to **focus** on _____.

2. My favorite **section** of a supermarket/department store

   _____.

3. The **location** of a store _____.

4. I know how to **select** good _____.

5. I really enjoy **purchasing** _____.

6. I like/do not like having a lot of **options** when I shop because

   _____.

7. _____ is a **considerable** expense for me.

8. I _____ read **labels** on foods because

   _____.

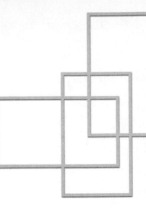

Section 2

EXERCISE 7 Fill in Word List 3.2. Practice the pronunciations of the words with your instructor or a partner. Write the meanings now or after you complete Exercise 8. Two items have been done for you as examples.

WORD LIST 3.2

Word	POS	Meaning	Example
aware		*conscious*	If you are **aware** of something, you know about it.
factor			Price is a **factor** in most shoppers' decisions.
research			Companies do **research** to learn what shoppers want.
conduct			Companies **conduct** studies to test their products.
technique			Different **techniques** are used in advertising.
affect			Price **affects** most shoppers' decisions.
benefit			Consumers **benefit** from lower prices during sales.
credit			Buying too much on **credit** can cause problems.
item	*n.*		You may purchase many **items** online or by telephone from catalogs.
constant			Consumers see and hear **constant** advertising.

EXERCISE 8   Circle the letters of the answer choice that has a similar meaning to the word or phrase in *italics*.

1. Many shoppers *are not **aware** of how* to compare prices.
    a. do not like
    b. do not think about how

2. Price is often the most important ***factor** in* consumers' decisions.
    a. reason for
    b. cost in

3. Market ***research*** helps businesses learn what consumers want.
    a. shopping
    b. study

4. Studies are ***conducted*** to find which colors and designs make products attractive to shoppers.
    a. done
    b. stopped

5. Point-of-purchase displays, near the cashiers, are ***techniques*** that stores use to encourage last-minute purchases.
    a. tables
    b. methods

6. Stores sometimes play music to ***affect*** the mood of shoppers.
    a. influence
    b. destroy

7. Consumers can ***benefit*** from understanding how businesses try to influence their decisions.
    a. have good results
    b. lose money

8. Many Americans make regular purchases with ***credit***.
    a. cash
    b. money used now and paid later

9. At a supermarket, the express line is for shoppers who have few ***items***.
    a. things
    b. children

10. Many stores have ***constant*** sales and special offers to attract shoppers.
    a. continual
    b. cheap

EXERCISE 9 Make flash cards for the ten vocabulary words in Word List 3.2.

EXERCISE 10 Read the two sentences below. Notice the uses of the bold words.

> Store decorations at holiday times can have a good **effect** on shoppers' moods.
>
> Long lines at the checkout stations, however, can **affect** them negatively.

1. Which is a noun? _____

2. Which is a verb? _____

3. How are the two words different? _____

Fill in the blanks with appropriate forms of **effect** and **affect**. You may need to change the words for number (singular/plural) or tense.

4. Brand or model names can have different _____ on consumers in different countries. One example is the old Chevrolet automobile model, the Nova.

5. When it was introduced, the name _____ most people in the United States very favorably—*nova* means "new star."

6. In Latin America, however, the name had the opposite _____. In Spanish, *no va* means "doesn't go"—not a good name for a car!

Benefit may be a noun or a verb. Decide which it is in the following examples. Write *n.* or *v.* above the word.

7. Having many choices is one **benefit** of shopping in a large store.

8. Businesses **benefit** from doing market research. Consumers also **benefit** because companies are better able to offer them what they want.

9. The directors of the corporation believed that it had **benefited** from the new advertising campaign.

EXERCISE 11 Decide if each sentence is true or false. Write T for true, and F for false. Then, change the sentences that are false to make them true. The first one has been done for you as an example.

1. __f__ Something that is **constant** happens ~~once in a while.~~ *all the time*

2. _____ We can learn about consumers' preferences by **conducting research**.

3. _____ A **technique** is a way of doing something.

4. _____ A carton of a dozen eggs counts as twelve **items** at the supermarket.

5. _____ Shoppers can **benefit** from sales and specials.

6. _____ When you buy things with **credit**, you must pay for them immediately.

7. _____ A **factor** is a statement that is always true.

8. _____ If you know and think about something, you are **aware** of it.

9. _____ How and where stores display items may **affect** consumers' decisions.

EXERCISE 12 Work with a partner or in a small group to discuss and answer these questions. Try to use the vocabulary words in your answers.

1. What is your favorite store? What are the **benefits** of shopping there?

2. What **factors** do you consider when purchasing something? For example, what **factors** would be most important to you in buying a car?

3. Think of a time when you shopped at a discount store. What **items** did you buy?

4. Do you have a **credit** card? What problems might having a **credit** card cause? In general, do you think it is a good idea to purchase things with **credit**?

5. Do you think most people are **aware** of how stores encourage shoppers to spend more money? Why or why not?

Section 3

EXERCISE 13 Use a dictionary to help you fill in Word List 3.3. Practice the pronunciations of the words with your instructor or a partner. Write the meanings in the chart now or after you finish Exercise 14. Three items have been done for you as examples.

WORD LIST 3.3

Word	POS	Meaning	Example
assume	*v.*		Some people **assume** that all Americans are rich.
conclusion			The **conclusion** of the jury was that the man was not guilty of murder.
alternative			Ordering online is an **alternative** to going shopping.
instance			There are several ways to save money. For **instance**, you can use coupons.
percent			Approximately 50 **percent** of Americans are female.
contrast			Black and white **contrast** greatly.
obvious		*clear*	His excuse about the dog eating his homework was an **obvious** lie.
required			A passport is **required** for entering the United States.
legal			In some states, it is **legal** for drivers to turn right after stopping at red lights.
traditional	*adj.*		Thanksgiving is a **traditional** American holiday.

EXERCISE 14 Read the passage. For each **bold** word, circle the choice in parentheses ( ) that is nearer in meaning.

AT THE DISCOUNT STORE

Do you really need five pairs of yellow socks? Probably not, but if a sign in a store or an ad in the newspaper says Five Pairs for Five Dollars, you may **assume** (think / hope) that you have to buy five to get the special price. In fact, many people might come to that **conclusion** (opinion / wish), but it is not correct. There are **alternatives** (good uses / additional choices). For **instance** (example / quick), you could buy one pair at one dollar. That is 20 **percent** (parts of 100 / not absent) of the product for 20 **percent** of the stated price.

How about some new shoes to wear with those socks? The sign may say Buy One Pair, Get Half Off on the Second Pair. There is a **contrast** (difference / similarity). In that case, it is **obvious** (clear / good) that you are **required** (suggested / obligated) to pay full price for the first pair. You cannot get the cheaper second pair without buying the more expensive one.

Is it **legal** (following law / being polite) for the store to confuse shoppers like this? Absolutely. It is a **traditional** (unusual / customary) sales technique in many businesses. It is the American way!

EXERCISE 15 Make flash cards for the ten vocabulary words in Word List 3.3.

EXERCISE 16 Identify the forms of the **bold** words by writing *n.* (noun) or *v.* (verb) above each one.

1. It is interesting to **contrast** marketing techniques in different cultures.

2. The **contrast** in the quality of the two products was very small, but the prices **contrasted** greatly.

3. Some people prefer to go to large malls or shopping centers; others, in **contrast**, prefer to shop at small businesses in their neighborhoods.

EXERCISE 17 Change the order of the words to write logical, grammatical sentences. Use each word in each group only once. The first one has been done for you as an example.

1. stores / or / holidays / after / It's / for / on / to / sales / **traditional** / hold

   It's traditional for stores to hold sales on or after holidays.

2. **assume** / regular / prices / lower / much / are / prices /You / sale / often / that / than

   _____

3. was / the / We / **conclusion** / best / came / item / the / that / cheapest / to / the

   _____

4. holiday / advertised / in / on / **percent** / decorations / department / off / store / January / 25 / The

   _____

5. sometimes / $500 / It's / you / almost / forget / $495.95 / **obvious** / is / that / but / it

   _____

EXERCISE 18 Circle the letter (*a* or *b*) of the answer choice that better agrees with the meaning of the numbered sentence.

1. The low price made the compact car the **obvious** choice for us.
   a. The compact car was the one we liked better than the others.
   b. It was clear that the compact car was the one we should buy.

2. The poor quality of the chair **contrasted** greatly with its price.
   a. The price of the chair was low.
   b. The price of the chair was high.

3. If you do not like this discount store, there are **alternatives**.
   a. There are other discount stores to shop in.
   b. This is the only discount store to shop in.

4. We **assumed** that we could return the item we bought on sale.
   a. We knew that we could return the item.
   b. We believed that we could return the item.

5. It is not **legal** for a business to advertise prices it does not offer.
   a. Businesses that advertise prices they do not offer can get into trouble with the law.
   b. Businesses that advertise prices they do not offer will not get into trouble with the law.

6. American consumers purchase many kitchen appliances. For **instance**, toasters, food processors, and microwave ovens are commonly found in American homes.
   a. Toasters, food processors, and microwave ovens are the most common appliances that Americans buy.
   b. Toasters, food processors, and microwave ovens are examples of appliances that Americans buy.

7. Stores in some states are **required** to charge sales tax on items they sell.
   a. Stores in some states can charge sales tax if they want to.
   b. Stores in some states must charge sales tax.

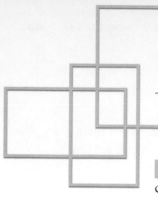

Section 4

CHAPTER 3 REVIEW

EXERCISE 19 Test yourself or a classmate by using the thirty flash cards you made for the vocabulary words in this chapter.

EXERCISE 20 Fill in the blanks with the best choices from the word bank. You may need to change the forms of nouns (for number) and verbs (for tense, form, or number). Do not use the same choice twice. The first one has been done for you as an example.

location	purchase	item	percent
select	section	identify	option
instance	alternative	conduct	credit
conclusion	considerable	label	

1. There are several ___alternatives___ to paying cash: writing a check, using a _____ card, or using an ATM card.

2. To _____ the best fruit, examine and smell each piece.

3. Store employees can often be _____ by their uniforms and name badges.

4. After several shoppers complained about the conditions at the store, city health department _____ an investigation. It was the _____ of the health department that the store had violated city regulations.

5. You can save money in many ways while shopping. For _____, you can cut coupons from the newspaper and use them to get special prices. Another _____ is to buy large quantities—for example, ten pounds of rice instead of just one.

6. What _____ of your money do you spend on clothes?

7. Shoppers who have many _____ in their carts cannot use the express lines at the supermarket.

8. You will find milk and cheese in the dairy _____ of the supermarket.

9. Gas stations with convenient _____ —for example, just off the expressway—sometimes charge higher prices.

10. Entertainment stores have movies and games to rent or to _____.

11. _____ on food products show you the ingredients in order from most to least. For example, if sugar is listed first, you know that the food contains a _____ amount of sugar.

EXERCISE 21 For each bold word with its definition. Write the appropriate letter in the blank. The first one has been done for you as an example. One of the lettered definitions will not be used.

1. __*g*__ **benefit**

2. _____ **assume**

3. _____ **factor**

4. _____ **legal**

5. _____ **require**

6. _____ **research**

7. _____ **affect**

8. _____ **design**

9. _____ **focus**

10. _____ **traditional**

11. _____ **constant**

12. _____ **technique**

13. _____ **contrast**

14. _____ **obvious**

15. _____ **aware**

a. clear
b. reason
c. continual
d. plan or drawing
e. conscious
f. difference
g. be good for
h. established through time
i. following the law
j. study
k. need
l. way of doing something
m. useful
n. concentrate on
o. influence
p. think

WEB POWER

You will find additional exercises related to the content in this chapter at **http://esl.college.hmco.com/students**.

What We Wear

In this chapter, you will

- Become familiar with twenty-two academic vocabulary words
- Practice choosing among multiple meanings of words
- Continue to make and use flash cards to test your memory of vocabulary words
- Read about how our clothes reflect our tastes and attitudes and the societies in which we live

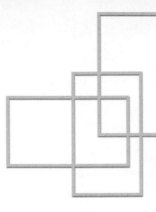

Section 1

EXERCISE 1 Use a dictionary to help you fill in Word List 4.1. One of the words may be both a noun and an adjective. Which one is it? _____ Practice the pronunciations of all the words with your instructor or a partner. Write the meanings in the chart now or after you finish Exercise 2. Several answers have been done for you as examples.

WORD LIST 4.1

Word	POS	Meaning	Example
individual			In the United States, the freedom of each **individual** is important.
cultural			**Cultural** factors help determine what people wear.
context	n.		Whether we use slang or more formal language depends on the **context.**
role			Each person plays different **roles**: student, sister, employee, and so on.
sex			Most jobs are now open to both **sexes**.
demonstrate	v.		You can **demonstrate** ability in English by speaking and writing.
attitude		*state of mind*	A good **attitude** helps people succeed in life.
job			It is important to find a **job** you enjoy.

EXERCISE 2 Read the following passage. For each word in **bold**, circle the choice in parentheses ( ) that is nearer in meaning. Use a dictionary as needed.

WHY PEOPLE WEAR BLUE JEANS

You may believe that the clothes you select to wear are only a matter of **individual** (personal / divided) choice, but other factors are also important. For instance, the **cultural** (social / average) **context** (situation / book) in which we live plays a large **role** (game / part) in what we wear. In the 1950s, middle-class American teenagers of both **sexes** (male and female / romances) began wearing blue jeans as a way of **demonstrating** (saying / showing) their independence. Blue jeans contrasted sharply with the more traditional clothing worn by their parents. They reflected a new, more casual and more democratic **attitude** (point of view / height) because they were originally worn by outdoor workers such as farmers and cowboys. Today, blue jeans are worn by people of all ages on all kinds of **jobs** (work / trips), and many of these people are not aware of the history of their pants.

EXERCISE 3 Make flash cards for the eight vocabulary words in Word List 4.1.

EXERCISE 4 On each line, write the most appropriate choice from the word bank. You may need to change the forms of words for number, tense, or person. Do not use the same word twice. The first one has been done for you as an example.

demonstrate	sex	cultural	individual
job	context	role	attitude

1. Sometimes, our _____*jobs*_____ require us to dress in a certain way. However, after work we are able to wear clothes that _____ our _____ preferences.

2. In the United States, the color of clothes purchased for a baby is often based on _____. A girl is dressed in pink, and a boy wears blue.

3. Blue jeans were first made by Levi Strauss for miners in the 1849 California Gold Rush. Today, they are worn in many other work and social _____.

4. Bankers are expected to take a serious _____ toward their work. That is why they are usually dressed in suits. The _____ of clothing is important in their occupation.

5. Americans are well known for wearing informal clothes, but they often dress up for _____ activities such as the opera and the symphony.

Master Student Tip

When using a dictionary to look up word meanings, read all the entries. Many words in English have multiple meanings.

EXERCISE 5 Read the lettered meanings of the verb *demonstrate* below. Then, write the letter of the meaning that best corresponds to its use in each sentence. Use each letter only once. The first one has been done for you as an example.

demonstrate

a. To show clearly
b. To prove; show to be true
c. To describe or explain by experiment
d. To take part in a public display of opinion

1. ___c___ The salesman **demonstrated** the detergent by removing blood and grass stains from a white T-shirt with it.

2. _____ The marchers were **demonstrating** for an increase in the minimum wage.

3. _____ People **demonstrate** their respect for a judge by standing up when he or she enters the courtroom.

4. _____ In 1522, one of Magellan's ships **demonstrated** that Earth was not flat by sailing around it.

EXERCISE 6 Discuss the questions with a partner or small group. Try to use the **bold** vocabulary words in your answers.

1. Baby boys and baby girls are often dressed in different colors. In what other ways does **sex** determine what males and females wear in the United States and in other parts of the world?

2. At the first Academy Awards ceremony after the terrorist attacks of September 11, 2001, most American movie stars wore simpler and darker clothes than in the past. Their clothes reflected the country's **attitude** at that time. Can you think of other ways in which an **attitude** has determined the way people dress in a particular place and time in history?

3. Clothes can express **cultural** identity. For instance, men in Scotland may wear kilts (plaid skirts) to **demonstrate** pride in their nation and in their history. What other examples of such clothes do you know?

4. How does the **context** influence what you wear? How do you dress for different situations and why? Consider what you wear to class, to work, on holidays, or on special occasions, such as birthday parties, weddings, and funerals.

5. What do you like to wear? How do your clothes and accessories (shoes, jewelry, hats, etc.) reflect your **individual** preferences?

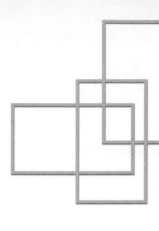

Section 2

EXERCISE 7 Fill in Word List 4.2. Use a dictionary if needed. Practice the pronunciations of all the words with your instructor or a partner. You may write the meanings in the chart now or wait until you finish Exercise 8. Several answers have been done for you as examples.

WORD LIST 4.2

Word	POS	Meaning	Example
code			The American Bar Association has a **code** of behavior for lawyers.
economic			The **economic** situation in many Middle Eastern countries is tied to oil.
source	*n.*		The **source** of the Amazon River is in the Andes Mountains of Peru.
function			A cash register receipt can also **function** as a bookmark.
appropriate		*proper*	Black is an **appropriate** color to wear at American funerals.
region			Different **regions** in the United States have different lifestyles.
minorities			The **minorities** of today may be the majorities of tomorrow.

EXERCISE 8 Circle the letter (*a* or *b*) of the answer choice that better agrees with the meaning of the **bold** word as it is used in the numbered sentence.

1. In the United States, some elementary and high schools have dress **codes** that students must follow.
   a. Students must obey rules about what they can wear to school.
   b. Students may wear whatever they want to school.

2. Sometimes, **economic** factors determine what clothes people wear.
   a. Money may decide what kind of clothes people wear.
   b. People spend a lot of time shopping for clothes.

3. The clothes they wear can be a **source** of problems between teenagers and their parents.
   a. The clothes that teenagers wear can make problems with their parents worse.
   b. The clothes that teenagers wear can cause problems with their parents.

4. Clothes have many **functions**. They protect and decorate our bodies, demonstrate our social status, and express our personalities.
   a. There are many good things about clothes.
   b. There are many uses for clothes.

5. In the past, it was not **appropriate** for a man to wear a hat indoors.
   a. Wearing a hat indoors was something a man should not do.
   b. Wearing a hat indoors was OK.

6. In some **regions** of the United States, cowboy boots and hats are worn daily by men of many different occupations.
   a. Cowboy boots and hats are worn often in some parts of the country.
   b. Cowboy boots and hats are worn in some churches and restaurants.

7. Members of **minorities** sometimes wear clothing typical of their cultures and traditions.
   a. Members of the largest groups sometimes wear their own special clothing.
   b. Members of smaller, different groups sometimes wear their own special clothing.

EXERCISE 9 Make flash cards for the seven vocabulary words in Word List 4.2.

> **Master Student Tip**
>
> When choosing among multiple meanings of a word in a dictionary, first identify the part of speech. Then, look at the possibilities for that form.

EXERCISE 10 Read the lettered meanings of the word *code* below. Then, write the letter of the meaning that best corresponds to its use in each sentence. You may use letters more than once. The first one has been done for you as an example.

code

a. A system of words, symbols, or letters used in place of ordinary writing
b. A system of numbers used to represent a geographic area
c. A system or collection of laws or rules

1. ___*b*___ The telephone area **code** for downtown Chicago is 312.

2. _____ During World War II, an American Indian language, Navajo, was used as a secret **code** by the U.S. military.

3. _____ The building **code** requires that fire escapes be clearly marked.

4. _____ A five-number Zip **Code** is used by the post office to sort mail.

5. _____ The CIA employs **code** breakers, people who study and find the meanings of messages sent by spies from other countries.

6. _____ Medical doctors in the United States are expected to follow a **code** of behavior.

EXERCISE 11 Circle the letter (*a* or *b*) of the answer choice that better completes each sentence.

1. In _____ with warm climates, businesspeople often dress more informally than those who live in cooler climates.
   a. codes   **b.** regions

2. In general, swimsuits are not considered _____ for the classroom.
   a. appropriate   **b.** economic

3. _____ groups, such as Mexican Americans, may wear traditional costumes on holidays.
   a. minority   **b.** economic

4. The original _____ of a man's necktie was to serve as a napkin.
   a. source   **b.** function

5. The military has strict _____ for how its members dress.
   a. codes   **b.** sources

6. Clothes can tell us the _____ status of those who wear them.
   a. appropriate   **b.** economic

7. Teenagers are often the _____ of new fashions, such as blue jeans in the 1950s.
   a. source   **b.** region

EXERCISE 12 Change the order of the words to write logical, grammatical sentences. Use each word in each group only once. The first one has been done for you as an example.

1. what / **code** / A / rules / wear. / set / for / dress / is / of / to / a

   A dress code is a set of rules for what to wear.

2. us / **function** / our / keep / clothes / is / One / warm. / of / to

   _____

3. different / different / in / wear / clothes. / People / the / **regions** / United States / of

   _____

4. are / people / clothes / What / in / city / **appropriate** / for / your / business

   _____

5. don't / are / who / today / Women / **minority**. / wear / a / pants

   _____

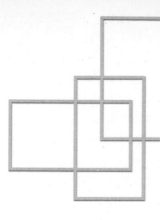

Section 3

EXERCISE **13** Fill in Word List 4.3. Practice the pronunciations of all the words with a partner or your instructor. You may fill in the meanings now or after you finish Exercise 14. Several answers have been done for you as examples.

WORD LIST 4.3

Word	POS	Meaning	Example
circumstances			After he lost his job, he found himself in difficult **circumstances**.
medical			**Medical** care in the United States is very expensive.
specific	*adj.*		*Fruit* is general; *apple* is **specific**.
corporate			**Corporate** employees work for large companies.
professional			Few athletes are good enough to play **professional** sports.
image			Because the factory polluted the air and water, its public **image** was negative.
similar		*alike*	Rice and potatoes are **similar** because both are carbohydrates.

EXERCISE 14 Read the passage. Then, match the bold vocabulary words below it with their meanings. Write the letters (*a–g*) in the spaces provided. The first one has been done for you as an example.

UNIFORMS

Children's uniforms in the United States are often clothes required by private or religious schools' dress codes. Uniforms ensure that children of all economic **circumstances** are equal regarding their clothes. In hospitals, **medical** staff members wear uniforms that are comfortable and easily cleaned. The military has very **specific** requirements for its uniforms, which indicate the branch of service (army, navy, and so on) and the position or rank of their wearers. Something like uniforms is also found in the **corporate** world. For instance, at one time IBM required its salespeople to wear shirts that were either white or blue. These colors were considered most **professional** looking and helped the company maintain a businesslike **image**. The shirts and business suits worn by these employees were all so **similar** that they could be considered uniforms.

1. ___*c*___ circumstances

2. _____ medical

3. _____ similar

4. _____ corporate

5. _____ specific

6. _____ image

7. _____ professional

a. different
b. relating to a large company
c. conditions; situations
d. relating to jobs that require study and preparation
e. relating to health services
f. related in appearance or nature
g. the idea that the public has of a person or thing
h. detailed; not general

EXERCISE 15 Make flash cards for the seven vocabulary words in Word List 4.3.

EXERCISE 16 Read the lettered meanings (*a–c*) of the adjective *professional* below. Then, write the letter of the meaning that best corresponds to its use in each sentence. You may use letters more than once. The first one has been done for you as an example.

professional

a. Relating to a profession
b. Showing specialized skill
c. Consisting of persons receiving pay; not amateur

1. ___c___ The uniforms of **professional** baseball players are made to order for each of them.

2. _____ In the United States, **professional** employees are usually paid by the year, not by the hour.

3. _____ Although she is not a trained chef, her dinner was very **professional**.

4. _____ **Professional** musicians sometimes have difficulty finding enough work.

5. _____ The report you produced looked extremely **professional**.

6. _____ The **professional** staff of a college or university includes faculty and administrators.

EXERCISE 17 Decide if each sentence is true or false. Write T for true or F for false in the space provided. Then, change the sentences that are false to make them true. Vocabulary words are in **bold**.

1. _____ "Large" and "small" are **similar** in meaning.

2. _____ The **corporate** world is small, family-owned businesses.

3. _____ **Medical** doctors in the United States work in hospitals, clinics, and private offices.

4. _____ The **image** of a politician is very important to her or him in getting elected.

5. _____ "President of the United States" is **specific**, and "George Washington" is general.

6. _____ Our **circumstances** are the situations in which we find ourselves.

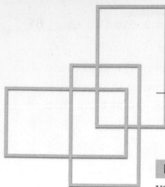

Section 4

CHAPTER 4 REVIEW

EXERCISE 18 Test yourself or a classmate by using the flash cards you made for the twenty-two vocabulary words in this chapter.

EXERCISE 19 Find and circle thirteen vocabulary words from this chapter in the puzzle below. Words may be read (1) horizontally (—) from left to right; (2) vertically (|) from top to bottom; or (3) diagonally (/) (\) from top to bottom or from bottom to top. One word has been circled for you as an example.

```
R U  I N D I V I D U A L
S E X D E L E M A N A T
M I N O R I T Y O N R A
I M Y K L A D C O D E S
M A X G R A W I S O N P
A G F R E M S O U R C E
D E M O N S T R A T E C
C O A B E Q U E R L T I
H R J F U N C T I O N F
Z J O B S F R O W G L I
L R M A T T I T U D E C
P A S R E G I O N N A S
```

EXERCISE 20 Match the parts to make sentences. Write the letter of the item that best completes the first part of each sentence. Sentences should be logical and grammatical. Vocabulary words are in **bold**. The first one has been done for you as an example.

a. how people dress.

b. wear business suits.

c. the **roles** we play in our lives.

d. depend on the **circumstances**.

e. people in a variety of jobs.

f. different **contexts**.

g. can indicate our **cultural** identity.

h. wear blue jeans.

i. that are **similar** to those of their friends.

j. wear easily cleaned clothes.

1. Our clothes tell others about ____c____

2. Uniforms are **appropriate** for _____

3. People dress differently in _____

4. **Economic** factors may influence _____

5. **Medical** personnel often _____

6. What we choose to wear may _____

7. People often wear clothes and hairstyles _____

8. Employees in many **corporate** jobs _____

9. What we wear on holidays and special occasions _____

WEB POWER

You will find additional exercises related to the content in this chapter at **http://esl.college.hmco.com/students.**

Coffee

In this chapter, you will

- Become familiar with twenty-two academic vocabulary words
- Learn about the role of regular and irregular verbs in academic vocabulary study
- Become familiar with some antonyms and how they may help you understand, remember, and increase your vocabulary
- Practice spelling vocabulary words
- Continue to make and use flash cards to test your memory of vocabulary words
- Read interesting facts about one of the world's favorite beverages (drinks)

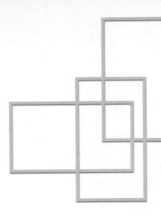

Section 1

EXERCISE 1 Use a dictionary to help you fill in Word List 5.1. Practice the pronunciations of the words with your instructor or a partner. Write the meanings in the chart now or after you finish Exercise 2. Several answers have been done for you as examples.

WORD LIST 5.1

Word	POS	Meaning	Example
estimate	n. & v.		Experts **estimate** that the population of the United States will be about 333,000,000 by 2025.
annual			Anniversaries and birthdays are **annual** celebrations.
stress			Exercise can help ease **stress**.
energy			Healthy young children have a lot of **energy**.
despite			We enjoyed our walk **despite** the rain.
positive			Parents can be **positive** models for their children.
issue			Birth control is an **issue** in some countries.
create		*cause, produce*	Artists **create** paintings and sculptures.

EXERCISE 2 Read the following passage. For each **bold** word, circle the choice in parentheses ( ) that is nearer in meaning.

MAGIC BEAN OR POISON?

Since its discovery in Ethiopia in the ninth century, the coffee bean has produced one of the world's favorite drinks. Coffee is so popular in the United States that, according to one **estimate** (calculation / respect), we drink twenty-five cups of coffee to each cup of tea. Worldwide, the **annual** (usual / yearly) expenditure on coffee is more than eighty billion dollars. Millions of coffee drinkers claim that relaxing with a cup of coffee helps relieve *stress* (pressure / work) and gives them added **energy** (happiness / power). Long-distance drivers and students preparing for important tests have often used it to fight sleepiness.

   Despite (although / and) these **positive** (good / bad) effects, the medical profession has always been concerned about coffee. The biggest **issue** (success / question) is caffeine, an addictive stimulant drug found in coffee. Caffeine can **create** (help / cause) dependence and heavy use, which may lead to heart, nervous system, and digestive problems. Because it is not clear whether drinking coffee has more benefits or dangers, most doctors recommend drinking no more than one or two cups of coffee per day.

EXERCISE 3 Make flash cards for the eight vocabulary words in Word List 5.1.

Master Student Tip

   Learning the antonyms (opposites) of words is one way to help you remember the words' meanings. Think of antonyms you already know, such as *rich/poor*, *short/tall*, and *teacher/student*. When you know antonyms, you can double your word power. (Keep in mind that one word may have more than one antonym, depending on the context; for example, the antonyms of *old* include both *new* and *young*.)

EXERCISE 4 Match each bold vocabulary word with its opposite, or antonym. Write the letters in the spaces provided. The first one has been done for you as an example.

1. __e__ positive

2. _____ stress

3. _____ create

4. _____ annual

5. _____ despite

6. _____ energy

a. destroy
b. laziness
c. relaxation
d. because
e. negative
f. good
g. weekly

EXERCISE 5 Complete the sentences by writing your own words and ideas. Your sentences should be logical and grammatical.

1. One thing I feel very **positive** about is _____.

2. _____ creates **stress** in me.

3. _____ is an important **issue** in _____ (name of country).

4. For a good dinner at my favorite restaurant, I **estimate** one would spend _____.

5. **Despite** the good weather, _____.

6. When I have a lot of **energy**, I like to _____.

7. I believe a person can live well with an **annual** salary of _____.

8. I admire people who can **create** _____.

EXERCISE 6 In each sentence, replace the words in *italics* with one of the words from the word bank. The meaning of the sentence must remain the same. You may need to change the forms of words for tense. Do not use the same word twice. The first one has been done for you as an example.

positive	estimate	stress	energy
create	annual	issue	despite

1. I drink that brand of coffee, and I have a very *good* opinion of it.
   positive

2. We did not count the cups of coffee he drank, but we *thought* it was about ten.

3. A little coffee relaxes some people, but in others it increases *nervousness.*

4. Just after World War II, the *yearly* consumption of coffee per person in the United States was almost twenty pounds.

5. Other drinks, such as tea and cocoa, also contain caffeine and can give people extra *power.*

6. *In spite of* the fact that cola drinks contain caffeine, many parents permit young children to drink them.

7. In cold weather, drinking a cup of hot coffee can *cause* a feeling of inner warmth.

8. One *topic* related to coffee production is the low pay of the workers.

Section 2

EXERCISE 7 Use a dictionary to help you fill in Word List 5.2. Practice the pronunciations of the words with your instructor or a classmate. You may write the meanings now or after you complete Exercise 8. Two answers have been done for you as examples.

WORD LIST 5.2

Word	POS	Meaning	Example
environment			A clean **environment** is necessary for one's good health.
method			Memorizing is one **method** of learning vocabulary.
labor			Years of hard **labor** went into building the Egyptian pyramids.
communities			Small **communities** generally have less crime than large cities.
physical			Both **physical** and mental exercise are important.
income	n.		We all need enough **income** to pay our bills and buy food.
conflict			When **conflict** between groups of people becomes violent, war may be the result.
resources		sources of wealth, support, or help	Computer labs and libraries are **resources** that some schools provide for students.

EXERCISE 8 Read the passage below. Circle the choice in parentheses ( ) that is nearer in meaning to the bold vocabulary word.

THE PRODUCTION OF COFFEE

Several issues are related to the production of coffee. Some have to do with the **environment** (natural surroundings / air). For example, coffee that is grown in the shade supports a wide variety of bird species, but few or no birds live among plants grown in full sun. For this reason, many people support the "shade" **method** (technique / location) of growing coffee. Other issues are related to **labor** (owners / workers). Although coffee consumers often lead very comfortable lives, in the coffee-producing **communities** (towns and villages / politics and economics) of Latin America and Africa, life can be very difficult, with hard **physical** (of the body / of the mind) work, little **income** (food / money) and few basic services. History shows us that violent **conflict** (behavior / disagreement) can occur when groups fight each other for control of important **resources** (natural riches / cities) such as oil, gold, and water. Sadly, areas where coffee is grown are sometimes also places of political unrest and economic hardship.

EXERCISE 9 Make flash cards for the eight vocabulary words in Word List 5.2.

EXERCISE 10 In the space provided, write the letter of the appropriate antonym (opposite) for each bold vocabulary word. Use a dictionary if needed.

1. _____ income
2. _____ labor
3. _____ physical
4. _____ conflict

    a. mental
    b. expenses
    c. exercise
    d. management
    e. harmony

EXERCISE **11** Decide if each sentence is true or false. Write T for true, and F for false. Then, change the sentences that are false to make them true. Vocabulary words are in **bold**. The first one has been done for you as an example.

1.   __T__   If you receive money for your birthday, that is **income**.

2.   _____   A group of people who live in the same place is a **community**.

3.   _____   The work of a college professor is very **physical**.

4.   _____   Trees are a **resource** for a country.

5.   _____   A good marriage is a **conflict** between two people.

6.   _____   "**Labor**" refers to the directors and owners of a company.

7.   _____   The **environment** includes animals, water, air, and plants.

8.   _____   A **method** is a way of doing something.

Master Student Tip

▼ Part of knowing a word is being able to spell it correctly. Writing a word several times helps you remember how it is spelled. You and a classmate can practice spelling by dictating words to each other.

EXERCISE **12** Put the letters in the correct order to form vocabulary words from Word List 5.2. Then, check your spelling by referring to the other exercises. The first one has been done for you as an example.

1. braol	_labor_	6. mnocymitu	_____
2. rcuseuoe	_____	6. vreonnneitm	_____
3. emdtoh	_____	7. slpyiahc	_____
4. moinec	_____	8. ofctcnil	_____

Section 3

EXERCISE **13** Fill in Word List 5.3. Practice the pronunciations of the words with your instructor or a partner. Write the meanings in the chart now or after you complete Exercise 14. Several have been done for you as examples.

Three of the vocabulary words are commonly used as both nouns and verbs. Which ones are they? _____, _____,
_____

WORD LIST 5.3

Word	POS	Meaning	Example
process			The **process** of doing laundry includes washing, drying, ironing, and folding.
available		capable of being acquired	In past centuries, green vegetables were not **available** in winter in the North.
remove	v.		Club soda will **remove** stains from fabric if used immediately.
major			Cancer is a **major** cause of death in the United States.
sequence			Introduction-body-conclusion is a typical **sequence** of paragraphs in a composition.
decline			A **decline** in employment means that some people lose jobs.

70

EXERCISE 14 Cross out the answer choice that has a different meaning from the **bold** word. The first one has been done for you as an example.

1. There are many ways of making a cup of coffee, but most **processes** begin with cold water.
   a. series of steps
   b. ~~machines~~

2. Today, home espresso coffeemakers are **available** for purchase in many stores in the United States.
   a. in place and ready
   b. expensive

3. Roasting coffee beans **removes** some of their bitter taste.
   a. moves again
   b. takes away

4. Coffee is a **major** agricultural product of Brazil, Colombia, Costa Rica, Angola, and Congo.
   a. very old
   b. very important

5. Coffee beans are prepared following this **sequence**: picking, cleaning, drying, roasting, grinding, and brewing.
   a. order of steps
   b. rules

6. Will coffee **decline** in popularity in the future? Tea growers are hoping that it does.
   a. go higher
   b. decrease

EXERCISE 15 Make flash cards for the six vocabulary words in Word List 5.3.

EXERCISE 16 For each bold vocabulary word, write the letter of its antonym (opposite). You will not use all the antonyms.

1. _____ **decline**   **a.** calculate

2. _____ **major**   **b.** increase
                                             c. unavailable
3. _____ **remove**   **d.** minor

4. _____ **available**   **e.** put in

EXERCISE 17 On each line, write the most appropriate word from the word bank to complete the sentence. Do not use the same word twice. You may need to change word forms for tense.

decline	available	process
sequence	remove	major

1. When you take a test in class, you follow this _____ of actions: First, you _____ all your books and papers from the top of your desk or table. Then, you choose a pen or pencil to write with.

2. The _____ of preparing coffee beans for use by consumers includes several steps.

3. Although some coffee is grown in Hawaii, the United States is not a _____ producer of coffee.

4. Dozens of types and brands of coffee are _____ at supermarkets and coffee shops.

5. Freshly roasted coffee is best. If you must store coffee beans for more than a week, keep them in the freezer to slow the _____ in quality.

> **Master Student Tip**
>
> Good news! Most of the irregular verbs in English are also the most common ones, which you have already learned—for example, *go-went-gone*, *take-took-taken*. Most new verbs you learn will be regular. The verbs in this chapter are all regular, which means you can simply add *-ed* to make the past tense and past participle forms.

EXERCISE 18 Write the past tense/past participles of the regular verbs below.

1. estimate ————————————
2. create ————————————
3. remove ————————————
4. decline ————————————
5. process ————————————

EXERCISE 19 Match the parts to make sentences. Write the letter of the item that best completes the first part of each sentence. Sentences must be grammatical and logical. Vocabulary words are in **bold**.

a. of tea and coffee.
b. **available** at most restaurants.
c. very practical.
d. from the table, it's time to go home.
e. much simpler than that of making coffee.
f. soup, salad, main course, dessert and coffee.
g. **declined** in popularity in recent years.

1. The **process** of preparing tea is ___e___
2. The United States is a **major** importer ————
3. Both decaffeinated and regular coffee are ————
4. The **sequence** of American meals is ————
5. Instant coffee has ————
6. When your host **removes** the coffee cups ————

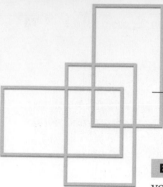

Section 4

CHAPTER 5 REVIEW

EXERCISE 20 Test yourself or a classmate by using the flash cards you made for the twenty-two vocabulary words in this chapter.

EXERCISE 21 Use the clues to fill in the puzzle. Be sure to check the spelling of each word.

Across

3. Of the body

9. Money you earn

10. Decrease

13. Once a year

15. Take away

17. Surroundings

19. Pressure

Down

1. Not because of

2. Question for discussion

4. Make

5. Work

6. Opposite of negative

7. A good thing to have

8. Disagreement

11. Town

12. Not an exact number

14. Way to do something

16. Power

18. Not minor

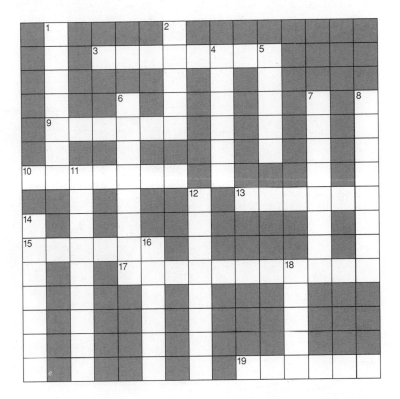

Libraries

In this chapter, you will

- Become familiar with twenty-two academic vocabulary words
- Practice recognizing, distinguishing between, and spelling adverbs and adjectives
- Continue to make and use flash cards to test your memory of vocabulary words
- Read about some important and common educational resources in the world

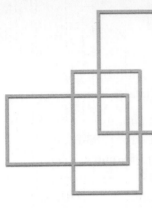

Section 1

EXERCISE 1 Use a dictionary to help you fill in Word List 6.1. Practice the pronunciations of the words with your instructor or a partner. Write the meanings in the chart now or after you finish Exercise 2. Two have been done for you as examples.

WORD LIST 6.1

Word	POS	Meaning	Example
established			The first daily newspaper in the United States was **established** in 1783.
documents			**Documents** such as birth certificates and passports should be kept in safe places.
journals			Professional organizations often publish **journals**.
assistance		*aid*	The government sometimes provides **assistance** to unemployed people.
residents			**Residents** of small towns are often friendlier than **residents** of large cities.
funds			Public schools depend on **funds** that come from taxes people pay.
sector			The private **sector** supports many charities in the United States.
criteria	*n. (plural; singular is criterion)*		Organization and grammar are **criteria** often used by teachers in grading students' writing.

EXERCISE 2 Read the following sentences about libraries. For each **bold** word, circle the choice in parentheses ( ) that is nearer in meaning.

1. Libraries are not a modern development. The most famous library of the ancient world was **established** (begun / continued) in 283 BC by King Ptolemy I in Alexandria, Egypt. It contained more than 400,000 **documents** (written items / employees).

2. University libraries have collections of **journals** (public organizations / professional magazines) such as the *Modern Language Journal, TESOL Quarterly*, and *New England Journal of Medicine*.

3. Librarians are usually able to give visitors **assistance** (help / information) in locating materials.

4. Public libraries are usually free to **residents** (people who live in an area / people who are from other countries) of the communities in which they are located. These libraries are made possible by **funds** (books / money) that come from local taxes. Additional money may come from the private **sector** (a piece of land / a division of something) in the form of donations by individuals, organizations, and businesses.

5. Librarians select items for their collections by using **criteria** (rules / laws) that include their cost and the space available to house them.

EXERCISE 3 Make flash cards for the eight vocabulary words in Word List 6.1.

EXERCISE 4 On each line, write the most appropriate word from the word bank to complete the sentence. Do not use the same word twice.

criteria	funds	sector	residents
established	documents	journals	assistance

1. Libraries may subscribe to and receive the latest issues of magazines, newspapers, and _____.

2. State and federal scholarships for college students come from public _____.

3. The Library of Congress was _____ in 1800.

4. Maps, letters, and contracts are among the many types of _____ that libraries may hold.

5. The performances of figure skaters are judged on two
_____: technical merit and presentation.

6. Mayors, governors, senators, and other politicians work in the public
_____. Getting _____ when it is
needed for the _____ of their districts is part of
their jobs.

EXERCISE 5 Write one or more words from the word bank to
answer each question. You may use the same word more than once.

established	funds	documents	criteria
sector	journals	assistance	residents

1. Which two words are things you might expect to find in a library?

_____

2. Which word is part of a librarian's job? _____

3. Which word refers to people who can use a local public library?

_____

4. Which word is something libraries need to buy materials for their
collections? _____

5. Which word can follow "private" or "public"? _____

6. Which word is important in deciding which items to buy for a library?

_____

7. Which word is a verb? _____

8. Which five words are plural? _____

_____

EXERCISE 6 Change the order of the words to write logical, grammatical sentences. Use each word in each group only once.

1. read / **journals** / scientific / Scientists

   _____

   _____

2. is / a / **documents** / library / other / A / collection / and / materials / of

   _____

   _____

3. local / **established** / Public / for / **residents** / of / libraries / the / are / use

   _____

   _____

4. **assistance** / deaf / Some / people / for / blind / or / libraries / provide

   _____

5. and / get / from / Libraries / **sectors** / **funds** / the / both / public / private / may

   _____

   _____

6. of / materials / librarians / select / may / Popularity / one / the / be / **criteria** / use / to

   _____

   _____

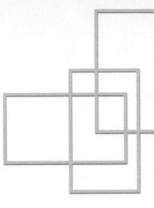

Section 2

EXERCISE 7 Use a dictionary to help you fill in Word List 6.2. Practice the pronunciations of the words with your instructor or a partner. Write the meanings in the chart now or after you finish Exercise 8. Two have been done for you as examples.

WORD LIST 6.2

Word	POS	Meaning	Example
structures			Understanding the **structures** of words can help you learn them.
primary			The **primary** purpose of a police department is to protect residents of the community.
evidence	n.		**Evidence** showed that the man had robbed the bank.
fundamental			Free elections are **fundamental** to a free country.
aspects			When making a decision, it is important to consider all **aspects** of the situation.
published			The first daily newspaper in the United States was **published** in Pennsylvania in 1783.
error		something incorrect	It is natural to make **errors** when learning a new language.

EXERCISE 8 Read the following passage. For each **bold** word, circle the choice in parentheses ( ) that is nearer in meaning.

THE LIBRARY OF CONGRESS

The Library of Congress, located in Washington, D.C., is the largest library in the world. Its collections are found in three **structures** (buildings / places), each named after a U.S. president: Thomas Jefferson, John Adams, and James Madison. They contain more than 113 million items in more than 450 languages.

The **primary** (first and most important / first and easiest) purpose of the library is to serve the Congress of the United States; however, its materials are available at no cost to all people over high school age. In this way, the Library of Congress provides **evidence** (things that prove / things that exist) of one of the **fundamental** (basic and important / basic and expensive) **aspects** (problems / characteristics) of a democracy—freedom of information.

One common but mistaken belief about the Library of Congress is that it holds a copy of every book **published** (printed and for sale / written) in the United States. It does receive copies of those books, but it cannot possibly keep all of them. Another **error** (idea / mistake) is the idea that all its contents are books. In fact, it also houses a wide variety of maps, recorded music, movies, and many other types of items.

EXERCISE 9 Make flash cards for the seven vocabulary words in Word List 6.2.

EXERCISE 10 Respond briefly to each item.

1. What are three types of **errors** that ESL students often make?

2. When was this book **published**? (Look near the front of this book to find the date.)

3. What is your **primary** reason for attending or wanting to attend college?

4. What is one **fundamental** need of all people?

5. What kind of **evidence** might be used to prove that someone has committed a crime?

6. What **aspects** of English do you find difficult?

7. How many **structures** are at the college or university you attend?

EXERCISE 11 Circle the letter (*a* or *b*) of the answer choice that agrees better with each numbered sentence.

1. The Chinese were the first to **publish** books printed with movable type on paper.
   a. The Chinese were the first to read books printed on paper.
   b. The Chinese were the first to offer books printed on paper to many readers.

2. The **primary** purpose of school libraries is to serve as resources for students and teachers.
   a. School libraries' most important purpose is to serve as resources for students and teachers.
   b. School libraries' easiest purpose is to serve as resources for students and teachers.

3. Editions of famous books with **errors** in them are sometimes very valuable.
   a. Mistakes in famous books sometimes make them valuable.
   b. Drawings in famous books sometimes make them valuable.

4. Food, water, and shelter are among the **fundamental** needs of all people.
   a. Food, water, and shelter are expensive needs of all people.
   b. Food, water, and shelter are basic needs of all people.

5. When making a decision, it is important to consider all **aspects** of the question.
   a. It is good to think about all sides of a situation when making a decision.
   b. It is good to think about all the positive points when making a decision.

6. Your excellent composition is **evidence** of your good writing skills.
   a. I can see that you write well because your composition is very good.
   b. I can see that your composition is good because you work hard.

7. The administrative **structure** of a college or university often includes deans, vice presidents, and a president.
   a. Deans, vice presidents, and a president are parts of the organization of a college or university.
   b. Deans, vice presidents, and a president are important people in a college or university.

Master Student Tip

   Some adjectives can be changed to adverbs by adding -*ly*. Adjectives describe nouns. In the phrase "a large dog," the adjective *large* modifies the noun *dog*. Adverbs modify adjectives or verbs. In the phrase "an extremely large dog," the adverb *extremely* modifies the adjective *large*. In "The large dog eats quickly," the adverb *quickly* modifies the verb *eats*. Learning both adjectives and adverbs can increase your vocabulary. Your dictionary tells you which word families include both adjectives and adverbs.

EXERCISE **12** Fill in each blank with the correct adjective or adverb given. Then, circle the word each adjective or adverb modifies. The first one has been done for you as an example.

fundamental/fundamentally

1. A library is a _fundamental_ (tool) for people doing research.

   (It) is _fundamental_ in supporting research.

2. Because of an early error in his calculations, the mathematician's formula was _____ wrong.

primary/primarily

3. Although students in the class are _____ Asian, there are several Hispanic individuals.

4. _____, or elementary, education in many U.S. school districts lasts from kindergarten through the eighth grade.

5. Cataloguing books is among the _____ jobs that librarians have been trained to do.

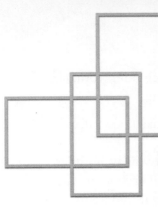

Section 3

EXERCISE 13 Use a dictionary to help you fill in Word List 6.3. Practice the pronunciations of the words with your instructor or a partner. Write the meanings in the chart now or after you finish Exercise 14. Several have been done for you as examples.

WORD LIST 6.3

Word	POS	Meaning	Example
goal			To graduate from college is a common **goal** of students.
precise	adj.		Architects must make very **precise** drawings.
task			Paying bills is my least favorite **task**.
complex			All languages are equally **complex** and difficult to learn.
potential			Everyone of normal intelligence has the **potential** to learn more than one language.
hence		therefore	The traditional, **hence** usual, Fourth of July activity is watching fireworks.
link			Computers **link** people who live in countries that are far from each other.

EXERCISE 14 Read the sentences below. For each bold word, circle the choice in parentheses ( ) that is nearer in meaning.

1. The **goal** (purpose / problem) of a library is to make knowledge and information available.

2. Despite the huge quantities of materials in libraries today, librarians must know the **precise** (special / exact) location of each item. The **task** (job / director) of organizing and cataloguing the contents of libraries is very **complex** (with many dangers / with many parts).

3. No one library can meet all the needs of every **potential** (serious / possible) user; **hence** (so / because), many modern libraries provide **links** (introductions / connections) to other materials via the Internet.

EXERCISE 15 Make flash cards for the seven vocabulary words in Word List 6.3.

EXERCISE 16 Decide if each sentence is true or false. Write T for true, and F for false. Then, change the sentences that are false to make them true. Vocabulary words are **bold**.

1. _____ If something is **potential**, we are absolutely sure it will happen.

2. _____ The grammar of all languages is very **complex**.

3. _____ Vacuuming, dusting, and cooking are household **tasks**.

4. _____ In mathematics, it is important to be **precise**.

5. _____ Preparing for careers and getting degrees are typical **goals** for college students.

6. _____ *Hence* is a synonym for *but*.

7. _____ A **link** is something that separates two things.

EXERCISE 17 Complete the sentences logically and grammatically by using your own words and ideas.

1. One **task** I dislike doing is _____.

2. One of my **goals** is _____.

3. _____ is/are really **complex** in my first language.

4. I believe I have the **potential** ability to _____.

5. Learning a language is not easy; **hence**, it requires _____.

6. _____ is one of the **criteria** I used in choosing this college/university.

7. Medical researchers have **linked** cigarette smoking to health problems such as _____.

Master Student Tip

Being able to spell words is part of learning them. Look back at Exercise 12 for the spelling of the adjective *primary* and of its corresponding adverb. What is the spelling of the adverb? _____ What spelling rule for adding *-ly* applies in that case? _____ Also in Exercise 12 is the adjective *fundamental*. What is the spelling of the corresponding adverb? _____ How many letter *l*'s are there? _____ The same rule applies for the adverb form of *potential* in Exercise 18. What is the rule? _____

EXERCISE 18 Fill in each blank with the correct adjective or adverb given. Then, circle the word each adjective or adverb modifies. Remember that adjectives modify nouns and that adverbs modify adjectives or verbs.

precise/precisely

1. A librarian must know _____ where items can be located in the library.

2. The man gave the police a _____ description of the bank robbers.

3. A piano must be tuned very _____ so that the notes sound as they should.

potential/potentially

4. Some _____ problems with a car can be avoided by frequent oil changes.

5. Electrical appliances are _____ dangerous to young children.

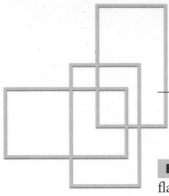

Section 4

EXERCISE 19 Test yourself or a classmate by using the twenty-two flash cards you made for the vocabulary words in this chapter.

EXERCISE 20 Discuss these questions with a partner or small group. Try to use the **bold** vocabulary words in your answers.

1. Nowadays, many college and university students must work and study at the same time; **hence,** they are often tired and their lives are stressful. Does this describe your circumstances? What other **aspects** of being a student are difficult for you? What can you or others do to make being a student easier? How can you **structure** your time to make the best use of it?

2. What are some academic and personal **goals** you have set for yourself? How will you reach your **goals**, and how long will it take?

3. Imagine you are going to buy a car/computer/house. What **criteria** would you use to compare and contrast the cars/computers/houses you are considering?

4. What **evidence** can show that you are the person you say you are? Are you carrying any of it with you today? Do you have other **evidence** of your identity at home? Are you a permanent **resident** of the United States? If so, what **document** can you show to prove it? What **documents** can citizens show to prove they are U.S. citizens?

5. Do you keep a **journal** or diary, a notebook in which you write about what is happening in your life and how you feel about it? If yes, what kinds of things do you write about? Why do people keep **journals**?

EXERCISE 21 Match each **bold** word to its appropriate synonym. Write the letter in the blank provided. Two of the lettered synonyms will not be used.

1. _____ **potential**

2. _____ **link**

3. _____ **task**

4. _____ **establish**

5. _____ **precise**

6. _____ **primary**

7. _____ **hence**

8. _____ **assistance**

9. _____ **error**

10. _____ **funds**

11. _____ **fundamental**

12. _____ **complex**

a. money
b. exact
c. help
d. complicated
e. special
f. mistake
g. connect
h. basic
i. good
j. start
k. possible
l. so
m. major
n. job

WEB POWER

You will find additional exercises related to the content in this chapter at **http://esl.college.hmco.com/students**.